DREAMWORKS

Spirit
RIDING FREE

Spring Beginnings

EGMONT
We bring stories to life

First published in 2020 in the USA by Little, Brown and Company.
This edition published in Great Britain in 2021 by Egmont Books

An imprint of HarperCollins*Publishers*
1 London Bridge Street.
London SE1 9GF

www.egmontbooks.co.uk

ISBN 978 0 7555 0132 8

71366/001

Adapted by Nikki Gamble

Printed in Singapore

Spring Beginnings

Attention, DreamWorks Spirit Riding Free fans!

Look for these words when you
read this book. Can you spot them all?

rears

pregnant

curtsy

waltz

Reading Together

Before you start reading, it helps to talk about
what you think the book might be about.

Does the title help you?
Are there any clues on the cover?

Sound out unfamiliar words and look for clues in
the pictures. Sometimes the words before and after
an unknown word can help work out what
a difficult word means.

After you've finished the story, go back to any words
that you found tricky and talk about what they mean.
This helps you to remember them!

Activities for after reading

Can you spot these words in the story?

protecting   herd   graceful   mare

What does each word mean? How do you know?

Question Time!

What is a ball in this story? What other types of balls
can you think of?

Advanced Question

How is Pru feeling on page 22? How can you tell?

It is springtime in Miradero.

The PALs, Pru, Abigail and Lucky,

race their horses across the frontier.

"I will win first place," Lucky says. She does!

Their race ends in a valley.

This is where Spirit's herd lives!

The girls walk toward

the wild horses.

A grey horse named Smoke rears
when the PALs reach the herd.
He does not look happy.
He is protecting something.

The girls see a pregnant mare.
That means the horse is going to
have a baby!
Lucky thinks they should check
on the mare again tomorrow.

Back at Lucky's house,

Aunt Cora has exciting news.

The new governor is visiting Miradero.

There will be a fancy ball to welcome him.

All the PALs are invited!

The girls cannot wait to go to the ball.

They need to get ready.

First, Lucky shows
her friends how to be
graceful on the stairs.
Abigail slips and falls!

Then, Lucky teaches
them how to talk
to the governor.
Pru is so nervous!

The next day, the PALs and Pru's dad
go to the valley.
They will check on the pregnant
mare.

Mr Granger tries to get to the mare,
but Smoke rears at him, too.
Mr Granger cannot get
close to the mother horse.

"There is nothing we can do,"
Mr Granger says.
"She will have her baby
without our help."

Later, the PALs continue getting
ready for the ball.

Aunt Cora teaches them how to curtsy.

She also teaches them how to waltz.

The girls are finally ready for the ball!

Just then, Spirit arrives!

He wants Lucky to follow him.

Something is wrong!

"What about the ball?" Abigail asks.

The horses are more important than a ball!

The PALs follow Spirit as fast as they can!

The friends reach the herd.
The wild horses are upset!
"We have to get to the mare,"
says Lucky.

She walks toward the herd,
but Smoke charges at her.

Spirit stops him and guides the
girls to the mare.

Pru goes to the mother horse.

"She is ready to have the baby,"

Pru says.

There is no time to get Mr Granger.

The PALs have to help
the mare by themselves!

Boomerang, Spirit and Chica
Linda stand guard.
Abigail keeps the mare calm.

Pru cannot take care of the foal alone.

She needs Lucky's help!

Pru and Lucky work together.
The foal is born!

Abigail hugs the baby horse.
"He is the cutest thing I have ever
seen!" she says.

The foal takes his first steps.
He falls down.

Spirit helps him up.
They join the rest of the herd.

The friends are happy that
the mare and foal are okay.

"That little guy needs a name," says Pru.

"I have an idea!" says Abigail.

"I bet it is Sprinkles," Pru guesses.

Lucky asks, "Is it Bunny or Gingersnap?"

"I think it should be Governor!" says Abigail.

The PALs all agree.

Governor is a perfect name.